Casey's CODE

Written by Gail Blasser Riley
Illustrated by Fred Willingham

STECK-VAUGHN
ELEMENTARY · SECONDARY · ADULT · LIBRARY

A Harcourt Classroom Education Company

www.steck-vaughn.com

Contents

A dit dah
B dah dit dit dit
C dah dit dah dit
D dah dit dit
E dit
F dit dit dah dit
G dah dah dit
H dit dit dit dit
I dit dit
J dit dah dah dah
K dah dit dah
L dit dah dit dit
M dah dah

N dah dit
O dah dah dah
P dit dah dah dit
Q dah dah dit dah
R dit dah dit
S dit dit dit
T dah
U dit dit dah
V dit dit dit dah
W dit dah dah
X dah dit dit dah
Y dah dit dah dah
Z dah dah dit dit

CHAPTER 1

Tryout Scare

Casey Okamoto stepped off the dock and onto Grandpa's sailboat, *Sun Sailor*. She was happy to feel the familiar rocking of the waves. Far across the bay, a huge ship was heading out to sea. She wished she could be on that ship, on the way to somewhere else—anywhere that would take her far away from school.

"I should have known better than to even try." Casey looked up at her grandfather and chewed her lip. "I thought I could do it this time. But the tryouts were just too much. I should have known I'd fall apart again. Every time I try to do something important, I just fall apart." Casey shuddered at the memory.

"Casey, there'll be tryouts for another play in the spring," Grandpa said with a smile as he ruffled her hair.

"But you weren't there, Grandpa. It was awful! It was like my mouth was full of marbles. I couldn't even get the words out. My hands started sweating, and then they started shaking so much that my script rattled."

"You'll do fine next time," Grandpa said calmly. "It takes practice . . . and believing in yourself."

"You know what else? We have to do an oral report for geography. We have to choose a place and explain to the class how to get there from our town. Grandpa, I hate oral reports," Casey said with a sigh.

"It sounds like we should set sail for the map shop," Grandpa answered cheerfully. He headed for the little cabin to get their life jackets. "Grab the line. Let's set sail!" he called over his shoulder.

The salty sea air nipped at Casey's nose as she untied the boat from Grandpa's dock. She breathed in a big gulp as they set sail. She was glad that she and Grandpa were going out on the boat today. The ocean always calmed her down.

Casey took a seat on a bench along the side of the sailboat and looked up at the sky. "Did you ever see a sky so blue, Grandpa?" She knew what he would say next.

"One time, in Japan," said Grandpa. "That was when I got to visit the city where my grandparents were born. They came to California in 1902."

"The Okamoto family has been in the United States for almost a hundred years," said Casey proudly. "That's five generations."

"Anyway, we were leaving Japan that day, and the sky was a clear, deep blue. We had no warning at all that a major storm was coming."

Casey settled back. She loved to hear Grandpa's stories about his days in the merchant marine. He had been a radio electronics officer on big cargo ships that sailed all over the world.

Grandpa took a seat across from Casey. "I thought we might not make it through that storm. The waves swelled around our ship like huge jaws about to take us down into the sea. Our radio equipment went out, and we were knocked way off course. At first I panicked. But then I thought about all the other men on the ship. I checked the charts, and I sent a Morse code S O S."

Grandpa tapped his finger on his knee as if he were tapping out a Morse code message.

"About that time," he went on, "a giant wave hit us. My chair was ripped out of the floor, and I went flying across the room. I never knew when I became a radio officer that there would be so much adventure—and so much danger."

"It's a good thing you were at the controls, Grandpa, and not me," Casey stated. "My hands would shake so much that I wouldn't be able to send the message."

"Don't be so hard on yourself, Casey. You can do more than you think you can. You're already learning Morse code. You'll have it down before you know it."

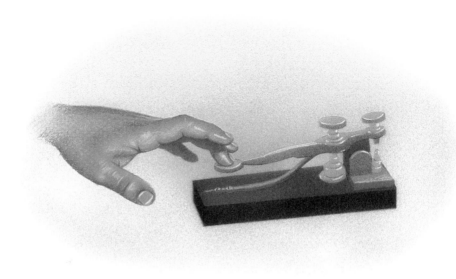

"Oh, Grandpa, it's so hard to learn. All those dots and stuff. And people don't need Morse code anymore. We have radios and computers."

"It's one of the easiest, simplest forms of communication. It works just like—" Grandpa started to explain.

"I know, I know," Casey stopped him in a bored voice. "It works like a doorbell. You push on the switch—"

"It's called a key," Grandpa corrected gently.

"Okay," responded Casey. "You press the key, and the electric current goes through and it makes a sound. You let go, and the current stops and the sound stops."

"Exactly! And each letter of the alphabet is made of a set of sounds. Dots are short sounds, and dashes are long sounds. *A* is dot dash, and *B* is dash dot dot dot."

"Right," said Casey. "That's why they call it a code." It always seemed funny to her that even though it was a code, there wasn't anything really secret about Morse code. Many people around the world had used it since 1840, when Samuel Morse invented it.

Grandpa got up. "I'll be right back. I want to call Ed Donnell. His ship docks today, just back from South America." Grandpa disappeared into the cabin. He called out to her, "Do I use the microphone, or do you want to try Morse code?"

"Use the mike," she called back. *Why is that old code so important to him?* she wondered. *We have wireless phones and computers today. All we have to do is call for help. Nobody needs Morse code anymore.*

A moment later Grandpa came out on deck. "Ed's ship is in. He's invited us over. Let's head over to the docks."

The Cargo Ship

Casey tossed the line around a post as she and Grandpa pulled in. The sailboat bumped gently against the dock.

"Hi, Captain Donnell," Casey called as she waved to him.

Captain Donnell walked over. "How do you like my ship?" he asked, grinning a wide grin.

She stood on the dock and looked up at the side of the ship. The smokestack seemed to rise straight up and disappear into the clouds.

"It's huge!" she said. "It must be a hundred feet tall. It's way taller than my school."

"Want to come aboard?" Captain Donnell invited.

"Yes, sir!" she cried. Now that Grandpa had retired, Casey didn't have much chance to go aboard big ships.

"The ship's sitting high in the water," said Grandpa. "Guess the cargo's been unloaded. What were you carrying?"

"Bananas from Guayaquil, Ecuador," said Captain Donnell. "They finished unloading a few minutes ago."

"The gangway looks really steep," said Casey, looking up. "It'll be a long way up to the ship." She grabbed a rail on the side of the gangway and struggled up. Grandpa and Captain Donnell followed.

"How did you do this for so many years, Grandpa?" Casey asked. "My legs are aching, and we're only halfway up."

"It's like climbing up four or five stories," laughed Grandpa, "but almost straight up and without stairs."

"Wow," Casey panted as they stepped off the gangway and onto the ship. "That was some climb." She stared across the ridged deck that stretched as far as two city blocks.

"This way," said Captain Donnell as he led Casey and Grandpa down a narrow hallway and through a small doorway. Red paint peeled from the gray metal walls.

"I know you want to see the radio room," said Captain Donnell.

"Sure do," said Grandpa, looking pleased.

Knobs and dials and a computer monitor caught Casey's eye.

"Look, Grandpa," she said. "Captain Donnell doesn't have a Morse code key. He has a computer instead. Morse code is like a dinosaur, isn't it, Captain Donnell?"

"Nope," replied Captain Donnell. "It's an old system, and it's worked for a long time."

Casey blinked in disbelief.

"We use computers," Captain Donnell continued, "but we keep our Morse code key as a backup. If all this other stuff fails, we can still send an S O S in Morse code. Morse code could save our lives."

I can't imagine all the other equipment going out, thought Casey. *Besides, I'd rather use a computer any day.*

"If it's okay with you, Ed, I'd like to show Casey how I used to work with the key when you and I sailed together."

"Go right ahead," said Captain Donnell.

Grandpa got out the key and plugged it in. Beeps sounded as he tapped the key. "Dit," he said to Casey as he pressed quickly on the key. "That's a dot." Then he pressed just a little bit longer on the key. "Dah. That's a dash. It's simple. You can make every letter of the alphabet with dots and dashes." Grandpa looked through books on a nearby shelf until he found one with the Morse code alphabet. He flipped it open for Casey and tapped out her name as he spelled it aloud.

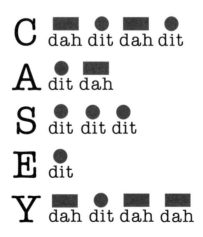

C ■ ● ■ ●
  dah dit dah dit

A ● ■
  dit dah

S ● ● ●
  dit dit dit

E ●
  dit

Y ■ ● ■ ■
  dah dit dah dah

"Now here's your last name," Grandpa offered. He began with *O*—dah dah dah. He tapped through the rest of *Okamoto* and turned to Casey. "You try it."

Casey squirmed. "Grandpa, you've shown me before. I don't really want to try it now."

Grandpa looked a little hurt.

Casey gazed out the porthole at the clear blue sky and the busy bay. She sighed a happy sigh and started to relax—until she remembered her project. Casey spun around on one heel. "Grandpa, my geography project! We need to go now. We have to get to the map shop, or I'll never finish in time."

"They'll still be open," replied Grandpa, looking at his watch. "And I'm thinking about a place for you to use in it."

They said goodbye to Captain Donnell and hurried down the gangway toward the map shop.

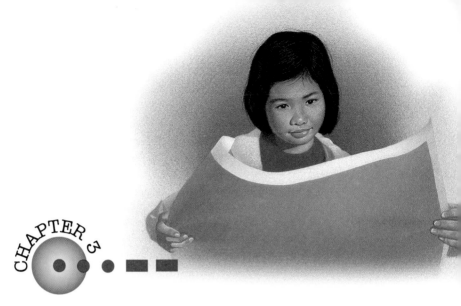

CHAPTER 3

A New Direction

"Feels like home," said Grandpa as he pulled out charts in the map shop and spread them across a table. Casey felt at home in the map shop, too. Grandpa had been shopping there as long as she could remember. There was something about the smell of musty old charts and new books that made the store very special to her.

"Look at this," said Grandpa as he pointed to a shiny telescope on a nearby shelf. "A telescope just like the one I gave you when you were five."

"I remember," said Casey. "You showed me the stars. That was when I learned about the Big Dipper and the Little Dipper."

"And I showed you how to use the stars to chart a course." Grandpa smiled.

"I wish things were like that in school," said Casey. "I wish you could give the geography report to my class. I'll probably just be old marble-mouth all over again. The map will get all sweaty."

"I don't know about that," said Grandpa. "You're supposed to tell how to get from your city to another place. What if you use a place that will really bowl them over? You can choose someplace no one else would even think of."

"Like where?" asked Casey.

"How about Guayaquil, Ecuador?" Grandpa pulled a map from a drawer.

"Where's that?" Casey asked doubtfully.

"It's a port on the Pacific Ocean," Grandpa explained. He pointed to a place on the map. "See, right here on the west coast of South America."

Casey thought a moment. "Isn't that where Captain Donnell's ship just came from? Where they got the cargo of bananas?"

"That's right."

"Oh, that would be neat," Casey said. "In my report I can tell them about going on the ship!"

"You can even plot two courses, one across land and one across sea," Grandpa suggested as he traced routes with his fingers across the map.

"Grandpa, do you think I could bring in some bananas for the class?"

"Sure thing!"

"Perfect!" said Casey. "This report might even be fun."

Grandpa turned to a spot down the counter. "Casey, look at this Morse code key. This thing must be almost a hundred years old. Looks like something they pulled up from a shipwreck."

Casey plodded over to the old Morse code key with Grandpa. The silver base was rusting, and the brass was turning brown. She didn't think it looked interesting.

Grandpa let out a whistle. He looked as though he'd never seen anything quite so beautiful in all his life.

"Listen," he said. The key made little clicks as he sounded out Morse code.

"That's *Casey.*" Grandpa clicked out *Okamoto.*
"Try it," he urged. He pushed the key toward her.

C dah dit dah dit
A dit dah
S dit dit dit
E dit
Y dah dit dah dah

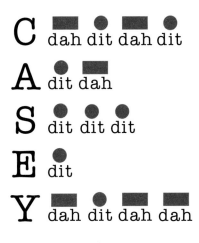

Casey knew this meant a lot to her grandfather. She reluctantly reached for the Morse code key. Something else caught her eye. "See that compass, Grandpa? It's just like the one that was on the boat when you first bought it."

Casey raced over to a nearby counter and gazed at the compass in its case lined with dark blue velvet. The gold arrows gleamed against the white face and the bold black letters. "After the compass broke and washed overboard, I never thought we'd see another one like it. I can't believe it!"

"Looks like this one's a keeper," Grandpa told the store owner. He paid for the compass and the map and handed them to Casey. They headed for the sailboat.

CHAPTER 4

Out of the Blue

Once aboard Grandpa's boat, Casey dashed into the cabin and pulled a screwdriver from a cabinet. Grandpa fiddled with the dials on the radio as Casey put the compass exactly where the old one had been. She took the small compass she and Grandpa had been using and slid it into the cabinet alongside the screwdriver. "We'll keep the old compass for a backup," she said.

"I'm going to call Ed," said Grandpa, reaching for his Morse code key. "I want to tell him about the old key we saw in the map shop."

Casey watched as Grandpa sent a Morse code message to Captain Donnell. "Grandpa, why don't you just use the microphone on the radio? Wouldn't you rather *talk* to Captain Donnell?" she asked, shaking her head.

"What would be the fun in that?" asked Grandpa, slipping on his lifejacket and tossing one to Casey.

Casey sat at a table in the cabin and laid out her new map. She listened to the rhythm of Grandpa's Morse code dits and dahs in the background as she plotted the course from California to Ecuador for her geography report.

Grandpa stood up. "I told Captain Donnell that you were using his ship in your report. He was pleased." Grandpa smiled at Casey. "Come on, let's get sailing."

Casey helped with the sails. When they were away from land, they sat on deck. "Tell me another sea story," she said.

"Remember my trip to Nicaragua after the big earthquake?" Grandpa asked.

Casey nodded. "You were one of the first radio operators to hear the messages asking for help. I couldn't believe the pictures you brought back. I felt so sorry for the people. Their homes were gone, and they looked so sad. I'm glad you're my grandfather," she said as she gave him a hug.

"I was glad I could help," he replied. "And I'm glad you're my granddaughter."

Casey heard the seagull cries overhead and looked up. She watched the graceful birds as they winged their way across the sky.

Scratching noises came from the radio in the cabin. "That might be Ed," said Grandpa.

"Can I tell him our position?" Casey asked.

"Fine with me," he answered. "Why don't you send it in Morse code?"

Casey laughed. "Nope. I'm a modern sailor. I'll use the radio." She picked up the microphone and radioed their position. Then she joined Grandpa on deck.

As Casey and Grandpa sat talking and watching the waves, dark clouds started to form. Distant rumbles gave way to a lightning bolt that streaked across the sky.

"Where'd that come from?" asked Casey. "I didn't see any storm warnings for today."

"Neither did I," replied Grandpa, looking up at the sky with a narrowed gaze.

Before Casey could say another word, lightning forked across the horizon again. The clear blue in the sky gave way to grays and greens. Thunder grumbled in the distance. Wind whipped tangy seawater across Casey's face and into her mouth.

"Help me secure the boat!" Grandpa shouted above the wind. "Then get inside! I think we're in for a storm!"

CHAPTER 5

Fear at Sea

Brilliant streaks of lightning raced across the sky. Thunder cracked loud and long. Then the rain came in hard pellets that stung Casey's hands as she helped tie down everything on the boat.

Over the roar of thunder and wind, Casey thought she heard Grandpa shouting for her. She raced out to see him pulling the boom of a sail toward the deck.

Grandpa pointed to another, and Casey reached out for the long wooden piece at the bottom of the sail, securing it with a hook. She couldn't believe how the weather had changed in such a short time. Huge white-capped waves crashed onto the deck, drenching her. The boat rocked fiercely. Casey's ears ached from the roar of the wind. Her heart pounded so hard that she thought it would leap out of her chest. She spat out seawater and wiped her mouth with her hand.

Casey thought she heard a thud pierce the roar of the wind and the smacking of the rain. She jerked around to see a loose sail swinging by the side of the boat.

Grandpa lay on the deck, his eyes closed.

Casey bolted to Grandpa's side and fell to her knees. "Grandpa!" she shouted. "Grandpa!"

Grandpa didn't move.

Casey saw Grandpa's glasses on the deck. Gently she placed them back on Grandpa's face. Her head boomed with each crack of thunder. The saltwater stung her eyes. The howling wind snatched her breath away.

The loose sail swung back toward Casey. Quickly she jumped up. She grabbed the sail, snapping it down and securing it in one motion. She dashed back to Grandpa's side.

I have to get Grandpa into the cabin! The words raced through her mind as she locked her elbows under Grandpa's arms to drag him to safety. "Wake up, Grandpa!" she called. But his eyes didn't open.

Casey pulled with all of her strength, but Grandpa didn't budge. *He's too heavy,* she said to herself in despair. She looked around wildly. *What can I use to pull him?*

She remembered the blankets in the cabin. *A blanket will work,* she thought. She slid a blanket under Grandpa, rolling him sideways and pushing and pulling at it while the rain and waves pelted her. She felt waterlogged from head to toe.

Casey braced herself against the wind and pulled on the blanket with all her might. Her fingers ached, but she kept her grip. Ever so slowly, the blanket began to move. Using it like a sled, Casey pulled Grandpa into the cabin and out of the wind and rain.

Inside the cabin Casey covered Granda with a warm dry blanket. The rain and waves pounded against the cabin door. She turned to the compass to check direction. The storm had blown them off course, and Grandpa was hurt. She needed to get help.

Casey turned to the radio. She flipped it on, and the power light glowed green. Then she flipped the microphone on. Nothing happened.

Oh, no! Casey thought. *It can't be broken. It has to work! It has to! I have to send for help. Grandpa needs a doctor!*

Casey grabbed the microphone. Her fingers felt like ten icicles. She shivered, scared and cold. She flipped the switch on the microphone back and forth, but nothing lit up. The mike was dead.

CHAPTER 6

Breaking the Code

Casey said to herself *The storm's tearing up the ship, we're off course, Grandpa's hurt, and the microphone's dead.* Casey started to shake all over. She fell to her knees next to Grandpa.

"Please, Grandpa, wake up. I need you. You'll know what to do. I'm scared, Grandpa, so scared. Help me!" Casey hung her head and sobbed.

But Grandpa didn't open his eyes. Casey saw his chest rising and falling. She knew that meant he was still alive, but she also knew he needed a doctor all the same.

The sailboat felt like a tiny cup tossed about in the huge ocean. Casey wondered how much longer the boat would last in the storm. *What can I do?* she asked herself. *I have to get help.*

Casey checked the microphone again. It was still dead. Her eyes fell on the Morse code key.

She remembered Captain Donnell saying that Morse code was a backup for times when modern equipment failed.

She reached out a shaky hand to touch the Morse code key. Slowly she pressed down on the key. It sounded a long high-pitched tone. *Dah,* she thought. *That's a dash.* She pressed again, quickly this time. *Dit. That's a dot.*

Casey breathed a huge sigh of relief. The key wasn't dead! It worked!

The rain hammered harder at the boat. Casey gripped a hand rail as a huge wave almost rolled the ship over.

She looked at her watch. It read 2:00 P.M., but it was black as coal outside. She switched on the boat's lights. They pierced pinholes in the terrifying darkness.

Casey's brain raced furiously. *I have to call for help. What's the code for "help"? No, they don't say "Help." They use some other letters,* she told herself.

Letters, letters. What letters do I use?

S O S—that's it, Casey thought. *S O S means "help." Now what's the code for S O S?*

Casey pulled open a cabinet. Paperback books fell out in a shower as the ship pitched. Not one had the Morse code alphabet.

She heard a ripping sound outside the cabin. A sail was loose. She knew she couldn't get the boat home on her own. She had to remember the code, and she had to remember it now!

Casey closed her eyes. Grandpa had shown her how to spell her name. In her mind she watched his fingers click out the letters.

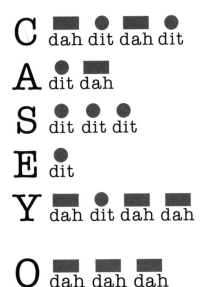

C dah dit dah dit

A dit dah

S dit dit dit

E dit

Y dah dit dah dah

O dah dah dah

Using the code for her name, Casey figured out the code for S O S. She reached for the key.

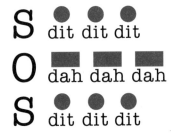

S dit dit dit

O dah dah dah

S dit dit dit

The first time Casey tried to tap out the
S O S, her hands shook, and she held the key
down too long. *That's not a dit. That's a dah. Do
it again,* she commanded herself. *Slowly and
carefully. Do it again until you get it right.*

Over and over she sent the Morse code.

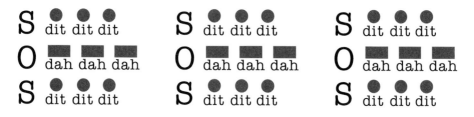

Would anyone hear her call?

CHAPTER 7

Heading Home

A voice came back over the radio. She couldn't make out the words. But someone had heard her! Casey jumped and yelled in relief.

She sat next to Grandpa to wait for help. It seemed like forever. At last, in the distance she saw a point of light growing larger. Soon the entire sailboat was lit by the beam of a huge searchlight.

A Coast Guard boat pulled up. Two Coast Guard sailors lifted Grandpa onto a stretcher. Others worked quickly in the driving rain to tie Grandpa's sailboat to their big boat. Once the sailboat was steady, a woman in a uniform climbed aboard. She smiled at Casey as she checked everything out. "Good thing you sent the S O S when you did," she said. "You're taking on a lot of water."

An hour later the Coast Guard boat reached the harbor, where an ambulance was waiting for them. Casey heard Grandpa moan. "Oh, my head!" he whispered hoarsely. "What happened?"

"The storm," Casey said. "The boom hit you. It whipped around and knocked you out."

Two emergency medical workers bent down to check Grandpa out. "That's quite a kid you've got there," said one of them to Grandpa. "She sent an S O S in Morse code."

"Morse code?" asked Grandpa. "Why didn't you use the radio?"

"The microphone went dead. It wouldn't work."

Grandpa reached to the back of his head. "Ouch! It's going to be a big bump. All my years at sea, and nothing knocked me out. I was always the one radioing help messages for everyone else. Now I get knocked out on my own sailboat." He smiled at Casey. "See? You *can* handle an emergency."

"Grandpa, I was so scared." Casey sighed with relief.

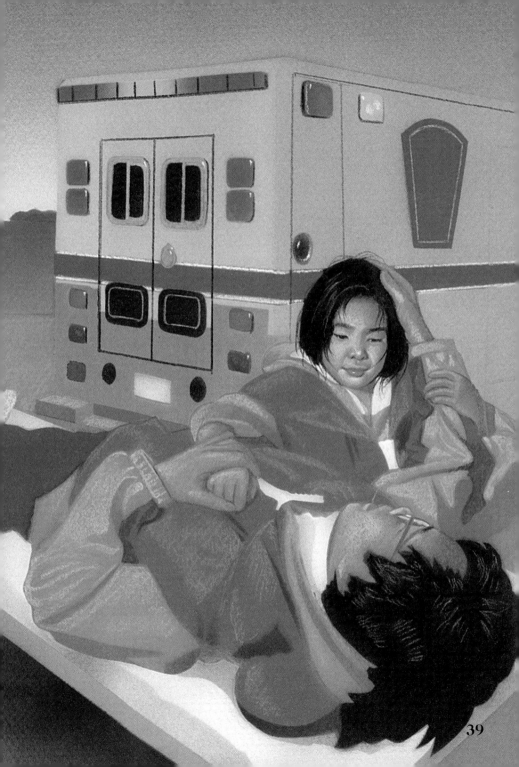

39

"Of course you were. Anyone with any sense would be scared. But you didn't let your fear get the best of you. You did what was needed. You sent the code and saved us. A real sailor, I'd say."

The medical workers picked up the stretcher. "You're looking much better, sir," one of them told Grandpa.

"Thanks to my granddaughter and her quick thinking," Grandpa bragged. "When the going gets tough, she really knows how to come through. And she knows Morse code. I'm proud of you, Casey!"

Casey grinned. Morse code wasn't so silly after all. For her, it was now Casey's code.

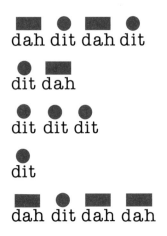

dah dit dah dit

dit dah

dit dit dit

dit

dah dit dah dah